Feelings
OUT LOUD

MOUSEY

Feelings
OUT LOUD

Emotional pulsations inscribed

Feelings Out Loud
"Emotional Pulsations Inscribed"
By: Mousey

ISBN: 979-8-9855858-9-6 (Paperback)
eBook ASIN: B0BXMQKJBC

Library of Congress Control Number: 2023903904

Cover design and layout design by Quisqueyana Press

To order additional copies of this book, visit QuisqueyanaPress.com, Amazon.com or contact:

QUISQUEYANA
Press

Quisqueyana Press
Poway, California, USA
info@quisqueyanapress.com
www.quisqueyanapress.com

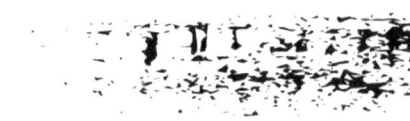

Table of contents

INTRODUCTION

The quotient is what is presumed as the love is divided into parts of the unknown; multiplied by the subtracted sensuality or lack thereof, which adds to the soul as these pages turn to pure emotions before your eyes. Join me on a journey beside my thoughts and feelings. Engage with my pen's letters as they spill ink-filled syllables, forming characters behind your very corneas and creating noises you can feel, pausing and speeding up your pulse with a certainty understood by few.

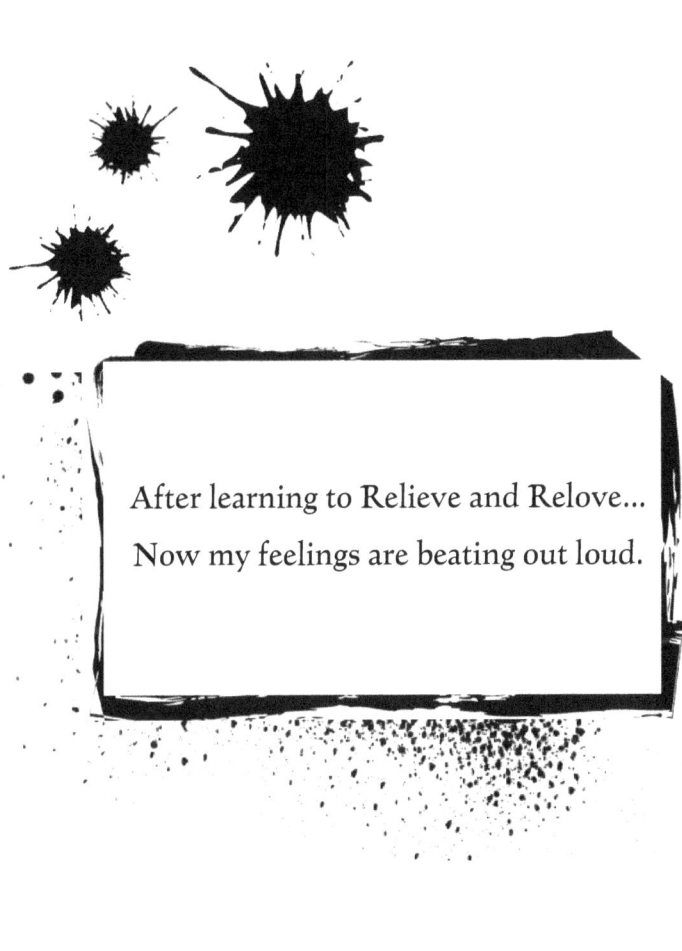

After learning to Relieve and Relove...

Now my feelings are beating out loud.

Who?

She doesn't know me. She glanced at my silhouette as my shadow interrupted her daylight, somehow irritating her as she read my mind.

She exhaled the more I chatted with her as I've tried to jog her memories with stories, nicknames, and favorite gifts.

She's so familiar to me as I've attempted to love her even while she's shrouded my thoughts with an uncanny smile during this attraction which kept my heart elevated.....

Pain

My head hurts; my stress level's reached an all-time high. My body pains me as I continue to host the mediocrity before my corneas, which would blind the average person. Pulsating thoughts rearranging what came to mind a second ago, causing a catastrophe once I've forgotten how to navigate through my dimension.

Pain reintroducing itself to coincide with the pressure beneath my skin as my blood temperature rises.

I'm losing my sanity while these jerks dance before the devil blindfolded.

Perfumed

Her fragrance haunts my thoughts.

I pursued her stride towards greatness.

I watched her glow with perfection while I dwelled in her shadows, impressed by her immediate professionalism strategies.

I often visualized her caressing my beard before planting her soft lips against mine, loosening my soul as she welcomes herself into my side, creating the image of total bliss as our pulses synchronizes almost immediately.

I've asked her repeatedly to stay beside me and allow me to appreciate her as she decorates my life. Kiss...

Lambs

Bruises can reveal the pain inflicted by beings mistaken for trustworthiness, especially at your weakest point during your trials in life.

Scars can serve as a reminder of your past pain during which you've had to make life decisions without said persons relating to your excursions.

Watch as my mind attempts to grow a cushion of fur as I shield myself against these so-called lions, revealing their lying done before their manhood could be revealed.

The surface of my mind is padded from pain inflicted by the very friend coinciding as a consultant towards foes to the side less trafficked.

Engulfing the world with propaganda; they prey on my demise in order for their lives to matter while they celebrate themselves in secret.

Tears from the sky

I like to walk in the rain, understandably weeping as no one can comprehend. Her selfishness, not wanting to help her elder, contributes as well as his desire to destroy anything in his path, looting and damaging at a moment's' notice causing a glitch above as a thunderous cry goes unanswered.

The downpour saturated my path, guiding me towards shelter from a flooded square filled with malice as they fended for survival from his mercy, which was unrelenting during this time of judgment as I glared in disbelief.

Stray dogs howled in anguish with visions of a warmed shelter as they drifted away once the current swept the vagabond bunch into the courtyard filled with debris.

Looking up, I could imagine his pupils dilated as the world let him down repeatedly, causing a nonstop flow of tears while the pain continued from scattered parts of life.

I've shed as much tears as he, but I've apologized as much as we.

I claimed imperfections ruined my search, but the truth of the matter was already with his focus during this trial by faith helping the world heal itself after disasters claimed the souls needed to regenerate his commitment to humanity.

Tears of an angel

I watched her; every step she took towards my life slowed my pulse. Her eyes displaced matter as she seemed to understand my pain, whispering a lullaby as she preceded to accept my thoughts.

Her mind absorbed as much as she could possibly while some clouds gathered just above her halo, which seemed to tilt like it was being weighed down.

She bore no resemblance to an average being filled with malice, although she grimaced in pain when she focused on my cerebral cortex.

Her tears reminded me of my pain as I've choked up all I could simultaneously with her bringing me to a state of rendezvous until I've crammed to understand me.

Crossed roads

Direction has become a means to prosperity towards the lives confused by false dreams.

The future holds no grudges once a choice is etched in ones' mind, alleging that was theirs alone.

Destinations are often confused as an intersection appears on the horizon as one is urged to choose while utilizing only recollection or second guessing as they neared the strenuous task at hand.

Dare I choose my own?

Two times

True love exists; his choosing to apply a lovers' reciprocity often suffers as his attention veers off towards distracting curves during his courting in an attempt to abduct his heart from his lovers' grasp.

Pulsating the moment his focus noticed her stride with a rhythmic flow, her lips summoned his tastebuds into the unknown before the eyes of his lover who blinked in disbelief as her fragrance disoriented his entire being.

Simultaneously controlling his heart before the mirror fogged up, she closed her eyes and frowned as he kissed her repeatedly before she opened her eyes to understand the reflection.

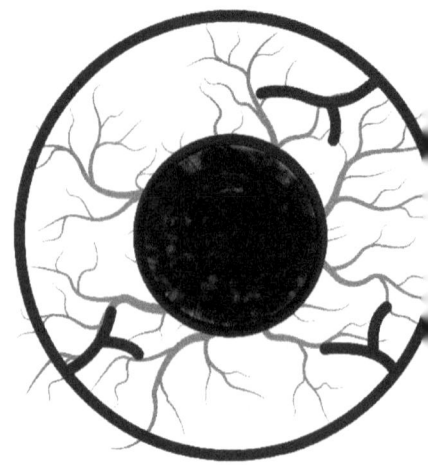

Sight beyond sight

I love the side view once you bring the worst to my attention; I almost forgot the wickedness you've announced beforehand, scoffing towards my reign as my courting your love was a mistake between our hearts.

I know now you were never special to me, detailing in full contrast how my love paled in comparison to your needs.

You deserve everything requested on your behalf as you complete your journey towards emptiness as the world observed the mediocrity displayed from the very lips I've kissed while being infatuated.

Filled in blank

She called me handsome; she adored my smile; she smiled in my presence while continuing to look forward to holding him as soon as I fell out of her focus.

She'd instigate a fault and dare me to defend my actions while she dreamed of being in his arms.

She left my love, allegedly seeking his acceptance, anticipating a reciprocal rendezvous to no avail. Looking back, she defeated exactly what she claimed mattered towards her future, as my wishes went unanswered.

I've surrendered my quest towards her heart as I've laid eyes ahead, noticing an ending similar to my minds' wishes as I puckered towards her arrival into new territory. Living by her side boasted a perfection like no other as my life seemed widen my smile.

Bruised ego

S he's misled, leaving me for who? You gotta be kidding me.

I'm not ready for what she has to offer.

Oh; I get it.

This is where I chase her till she succumbs to my persuasiveness and loves me as I've done this entire time.

I haven't heard from her as of yet, still I trek towards her heart, which seems more distant than ever.

They all smiled at my presence, unannounced, as my shoulders hosted the chuckles and snickers while watching my futile attempt to swoon her.

She smiled as I closed our distance almost immediately, waving me off as I cleared my throat. Gasping in disbelief, I glared at her stride as my posture defeated my stance once I felt the mild breeze from her fanning my soul away...

Loophole

I felt the loophole tighten against my jugular as they typed it into existence; choking my rights out of my very body during this alleged trial on my complexion, which commenced ages ago.

I've listened to my veins constrict, gasping to become relevant towards the plight I've been thrusted into chains, bonded with a similar shade once it oxidizes after being wrapped around my hands, restricting freedom simultaneously as I sank towards the bottom of the ocean as others stared in disbelief.

I could see the fear in their eyes from my watery grave as they were introduced to this loophole, reducing them to a third of what they possessed.

I could only imagine this feeling as they're led down this narrow path of enslavement while their wounds being only attended to with rays of the sun.

I've mourned as I sunk to the bottom of my excursion, exhaling the last breath while the salt water rushed me towards my end.

Sign language

You winked at me, beckoning my attention in an attempt to sway my feelings towards your aggressive behavior.

You ran your soul across my thoughts, waiting for my alleged reaction after noticing my pupils dilate wider than ever.

You blew a kiss once our eyes met, feeding your tuition as I focused solely on where your angelic body stood. Marveling at your beauty caused my pulse to strengthen as my heart pumped vigorously, keeping a destination of romance to which you blushed as I puckered, anticipating total pleasure...

Monsieur L. D. Mon...

Trois cents Francs...

... commerce ... le 31 Juillet ...

Paris le ...

Monsieur.

Broken shoulders

The fear of letting them down hurts my pride. The weight of my promises topped by obstacles before me threatens my succumbing, while my perspiration engages alongside the courage I've brandished.

Freeing my soul with a swipe of my brow, I've taken hold of a narrow future and toted my luggage onward. Jumping onto a ledge of regret, I've turned back only to witness my trail of advancements from my thinking process.

The problems of this world silenced my focus at first, now worshipping my stride as my past seemed to correct itself to my current state of determination.

Standing still

I will be back as soon as I'm done; I'll bring you your flowers when I'm on my way. I'll kiss you once I return, promising a steady future as the sound of a screeching vehicle shakes your heart on the other end of that phone, interrupting my promise to love you the way I've always guaranteed.

The Knock at your door is more alarming to your thoughts as you've noticed my keys aren't near yours.

The knocking persists, drowning out your thoughts as you see lights beneath your door blaring your focus along with the pounding against your mind before you deny the worst to come, reluctantly approaching your future alone as the knocking continued.

Your elevated pulse is now faint as you open your door, blinded by the glare on their shields as you wake up suddenly from this lifelike simile.

Gasping for the worst, you reached for my hand as the sheets hosted your touch.

You've glanced over as tears raced out of your ducts, begging for my return as I made my way out of your dreams, half dressed and grabbing a towel, to your amazement...

Considerable felon

She stole from me; she has no right. Taking what doesn't belong to her.

She should be considered a criminal for the damage she's done, carrying on her day as if nothing ever mattered to her while my heartbeat slowed as she kept it on her person, entertaining whoever she laid her beautiful eyes on.

Leaving clues for my eyes to decipher as I pursued a faint pulse before she smiled only a few feet from me, watching him in her peripheral.

Controlling my emotions and laughing almost uncontrollably as tears race towards my beard, wiping my feelings aside as I stared at her future without my love which stained my sight as her very fingerprint burned its way into my mind.

Handcuffing what she means to my savings naturally spent away from my investment bankrupted my love, watching her choose from the lineup made my lips smirk...

Unpackaged belongings

I have walked backwards as she denied loving me, retracing my mistakes. Walked with my head down as soon as her lips curled, and she remanded her heart verbally.

Backwards, I felt the thoughts of an adolescent repeating school directly after being scolded mercilessly. As I searched for a relevant factor, I pleaded with her to love me as she did before.

She rolled her eyes after exhaling for the last time, focusing on my tears.

She held my love at an advantage, destroying what I thought was shared between the union forged from scratch. Denied; only one sided as my efforts to seal our bond never adhered no matter what I've attempted.

Loving our relationship came at a price unaffordable by any means during this quarter, where we've been dealt to the world accordingly.

Me, not wanting to be lonely, asked for forgiveness, although my only admission was too much love invested in an endless cycle of greed and selfishness. Retracing my wrongs as my path was wiped clear with a gust of wind.

I've smiled politely with both hands in the air loosening my life as I've discarded the feeling she designed for my soul. My focus suddenly corrected itself, allowing my path to lead me to true love. Mistakes formed a line beneath perfection, with my love inherited solely by my willingness to forgive.

War of tugs

Reasons for trust shouldn't exist as I look to my left, noticing my friends' departure from my peripheral as I wonder at my future, unguarded from their protection as they reappeared in the stands applauding my demise which was thwarted by the friends on my right, barricading my life within theirs... only the appreciated need not ask for they are greatly appreciated for such actions.

Restriction

S he doesn't know what she wants.
She tells me all the time,
I know different.

She kisses my lips as she whispers to herself,
unbeknownst to my attention,
as I wanted to love her as she deserved.

She takes my heart jokingly,
pierces my love with uncertainty
as it drips directly beneath her intentions.

She gave me a chance to reconcile with her departure
during my pain,
to which no man can bear.
yet I stand straighter than most,

focused on the longevity near the horizon.
She used to kiss my lips
longing to feel my pulse rumble,
as our love ignited pure passion.

Now I've managed to glaze mine
as the taste of a sweet cream decorated her dimple.

I know but one path I've chosen
could grant my heart the very love to which I seek.

I will have to leave this empire being
that it no longer entertains my hearts' desire.

Rebranded legacy

My greatness is secondary to his stride;
majestic enough for the world to see and honor,
yet warm enough to cherish his offspring
as he guides us into roles of perfection.

His posture.
That of an immortal,
thoughts of a king,
conquering tasks at a moments' whim.

Hands made to shelter the meek,
as his grasp on this excursion
felt like the definition of an entire lifetime.
His love super-cedes naysayers,
overlooks those filled with hatred

as well as the foes in his shadows,

shifting in his presence,

overwhelmed by his brightness,

especially his ability to adhere to his truth.

Amazed

A m I the next coming of genius?

Am I who they see in their sights as they search for perfection?

Maybe I'm not what I think I am.

Maybe their curiosity led them to where I stood as I've illuminated their presence.

Could I make them better individuals who'd trail my thoughts continuously?

Would I matter to their truths if they never felt my pains?

Sounds amicable, although most would argue against my opinions as claims of betterment would loom over their past.

Hearing laughter amongst the wails supported my intuition as I stepped over their tears in route to my futures' history, titling me a gift in the making.

Un-excavated

I have buried my ego.

I've tossed the shovel aside with a passion known to a small percentage of beings I've had the fortune of knowing.

Learning to adjust to this way of life keeps me grounded, although I've often wondered if the world would have contributed to my strife had it been theirs. I've longed to accept the words gifted to my drive by my choices, illuminating the future I so desperately needed.

Hapless with my path, as my pain reflected agony and sorrow during a reconciliation involving the very fork I've chosen to collect against a different path.

Thinking Out Loud

Intimidating my heart with her beauty, I dared not compliment her at first glance, which slowed my pulse along with my stride as I've displayed the chinks in my armor caused by her aura.

I suddenly found myself apologizing for spending too much time appreciating her smile as her lips whispered, releasing a sweetened scent of a pale rose hidden between the pages of her story as I read informally.

Lustily I smiled as the ridges of her softly manicured fingers read my pores in anticipation of a relation built only for the strong minded. With every page, I've fell victim to her thoughts as her beck and call held me captive for some time. Finding my place beside her with a firm kiss planted reignited what we yearned for all this time.

Long were those days I've prayed for while she'd swoon with my every step towards her soul; how I longed to stare into her smile as she'd blush out loud whenever I'd catch a glimpse of perfection. She knows me too well as her ears stood at attention; I'll cherish her for the rest of my life as we stood silent, focused on each other's detail.

Bled less

I have lost my bandage, which kept my pain at bay from the scrutiny of the world. I'll work to make my value mean more than she's ever known.

Do you think she cares? The click in my background signifies her attention summoned by his every word diligently as she waves me off during this text session, which seemed to re-injure my pride.

I don't need this lack of attention by her shoulder blades keeping me company. Staring at wounds on my body. I've learned to harness crudeness from her very actions as the sun shined above my thoughts. Texting my farewell message to her inbox, I've logged out of her life once she's felt the breeze of emptiness host her narrow future.

Reenact

I have severed my hold on the very woman I've fallen for, but I can't seem to forget her as I long to hear her yelling at my tardiness or blaming my actions which led to her departure from my life, dragging tears down my handsome face and hoping to see a different outcome once she's settled in.

I could feel it cracking beneath my brown eyes once I've understood tomorrow and the pain, I've became accustomed to as I've paused before the revolving door, somehow remembering this similarity.

She chuckled from across the floor as if her cue was orchestrated before I could explain why I knew where she was before she chimed in.

Thin

This margin is virtuously unnoticeable, being its color brandishes the offset between the two. In some cases, it's overbearing, depending on circumstantial issues. Other cases often beautify the affection one displays as their soulmate appears on the horizon.

This line, thinner than one would ever know, has a durable layer somewhat impenetrable to most. They who came to know and respect it often chose the side related towards their soul as they seek to embrace what they've understood. As they've experienced heartbreak or sadness amid the meek spewing hatred, the world labeled them sourly as their pain converted their sadness towards the envy with the need to be relevant.

However, the few who remained steadfast in their pursuit of love resulted in sheer joy, unwavering as the embracing of gratitude continued to the wee hours of their lives.

Watching from the distance only fueled their curiosity coupled with mild hatred as they pled within themselves to enjoy what they've despised mostly for no reason at all as they stared at this line.

Intuitiveness

Cologne unfamiliar to my nostrils summoned an awareness before I could return a kiss to her partly glazed lips, our eyes focusing on each other as her nervous smirk told a lie.

My entire life crowded my thoughts suddenly, prying my ducts with an uncanny force as my pupils glazed over. Her pretty eyes couldn't bear the sight of disappointment as I've released my hold on her body.

I felt solely responsible for ousting this infidelity, as I've expected once she showed me a bit less attention. His name signaled a new beginning as she welcomed his aggressiveness while I've come to understand why my love never mattered.

Noticing the flesh beneath her manicured nails drew tears from my focus. I've receded into my heart's failure to adjust to a blackened organ, unable to live with the thought of loving ever.

Absentee

L ack thereof; almost a no show whenever the world would request my attendance during this participation from the deepest wounds in my mind.

Absence always sat in place during my reluctance to influence those in need to worship a struggle whenever convenient.

I've warned my future about my past as it caught up, somehow circling the present bearing presents of destruction from within the folds of my thoughts to contribute to pain in the path of perfection.

Was I able to thwart this menacing act as I've perished while I've arrived days later, staring at my past as my body seemed lifeless when I touched it?

But I've felt what I could only assume was pleasure as I've dealt a winning blow to supersede this victory, as chaotic as I could imagine this repetition would be.

Marking my life present could ruin the future destined, allowing my soul to grace the very cobblestones stained with my essence before my feet. My seat nearly warmed to the touch, welcoming what was already in place during my thought process, as my name was called the third time.

Manslaughter

I chuckled at the thought as I watched him tighten his lip as he pointed the interrogation light towards my eyes. Squinting as my dimples revealed themselves, I exhaled a sigh of relief as they questioned me over and over. I burst out again, laughing at the charges once I've read and reread the very document, missing a quotation between the first syllable following my name, miss-spelled already as if the actual case was legit.

Perspiration seeped through his fist as he slammed both hands on the table, causing the soda can to tip over. I caught it in time to salvage a swallow before belching louder than his negotiating tactics.

I've held my breath for as long as I could, refraining from correcting their mistake when he looked at the paper moistened with soda as his interpretation of the charge corrected itself in his mind.

Slanted

Her whispers interrupted my stride.

Her secrets detained my thoughts.

Her messages created my doubts.

Her creation ruined my trust.

Her unfaithfulness destroyed what I thought was perfect.

Her strength weakened my heart.

Her sorrow was worth my pain.

Her willingness to lie to me proved valuable to the minus the distance.

Her soul worshipped my departure as she despised my arrivals.

Her curves aligned my vision as secondhand as his was second to none.

Her needs to be romanced silenced my love for her finally.

Her strained focus cleared up as I walked away from this world.

My job interview

I have applied my heart to be loved by her approach; making myself comfortable behind her irises as her colored pupils warmed to my introduction.

I've granted permission to inspect my life before her demands while aimlessly wanting her to accept my flaws as is.

I've pondered deeply, watching her dissect my feelings as if my mind was an actual reference inspired by her thoughts of what she'll deem a loyal man. Slightly gazing at my posture over her glasses, she took a deep breath as to prepare a speech after clearing her throat.

I've sighed as she reached for my heart, welcoming my advances with a smirk as I could see her blushing while fogging her lens almost immediately.

Perfumed

Her fragrance haunts my thoughts. I pursued her stride towards greatness. I watched her glow with perfection while I dwelled in her shadows, impressed by her immediate professionalism strategies.

I often visualized her caressing my beard before planting her soft lips against mine, loosening my soul as she welcomes herself into my side, creating the image of total bliss as our pulses synchronizes almost immediately.

I've asked her repeatedly to stay beside me and allow me to appreciate her as she decorates my life. Kiss...

A host & a gesture

I need her to host my heart forever; she needs to understand my pulse as her name appears in my slumber.

We synchronized at first sight, unrelenting waiver to my love, which she's welcomed wholeheartedly.

I held her closer to me than my thoughts as I partially mistaken her kiss for an invitation to her soul to which was being occupied by my presence.

I can do this for the rest of my natural life even as she yawns.

Current she

Her curves are that of chiseled perfection; defined by her stride as she chooses her oracle in hopes of security, knowing that her enjoyment lasts as long as the breath she's taken during each night laced with disappointment.

Over and over, she's chosen said persons as concubines for a price as she supports her wellbeing with the proceeds.

Downward she spirals, losing her faith in humanity aside from the assortment of males paying for a night of pleasure as she reminisces on compliments given by the one true individual whose ever noticed her high cheekbones beneath her tears.

Passersby

Love happens naturally; love keeps your focus intact once someone initiates attention with the smallest gesture towards your pulse in an attempt to secure a bond with you.

Love stifles your senses as you sacrifice your entire soul to actually mesh with your mate, who happens to be focused elsewhere simultaneously as you hold hands. Falsely claiming pure trust as the alleged windows to their soul bear a shocking resemblance to a bare cupboard.

Unfair; yet the heart being separate from the brain creates a need to be wanted simultaneously as their signals pass each like strangers in the night.

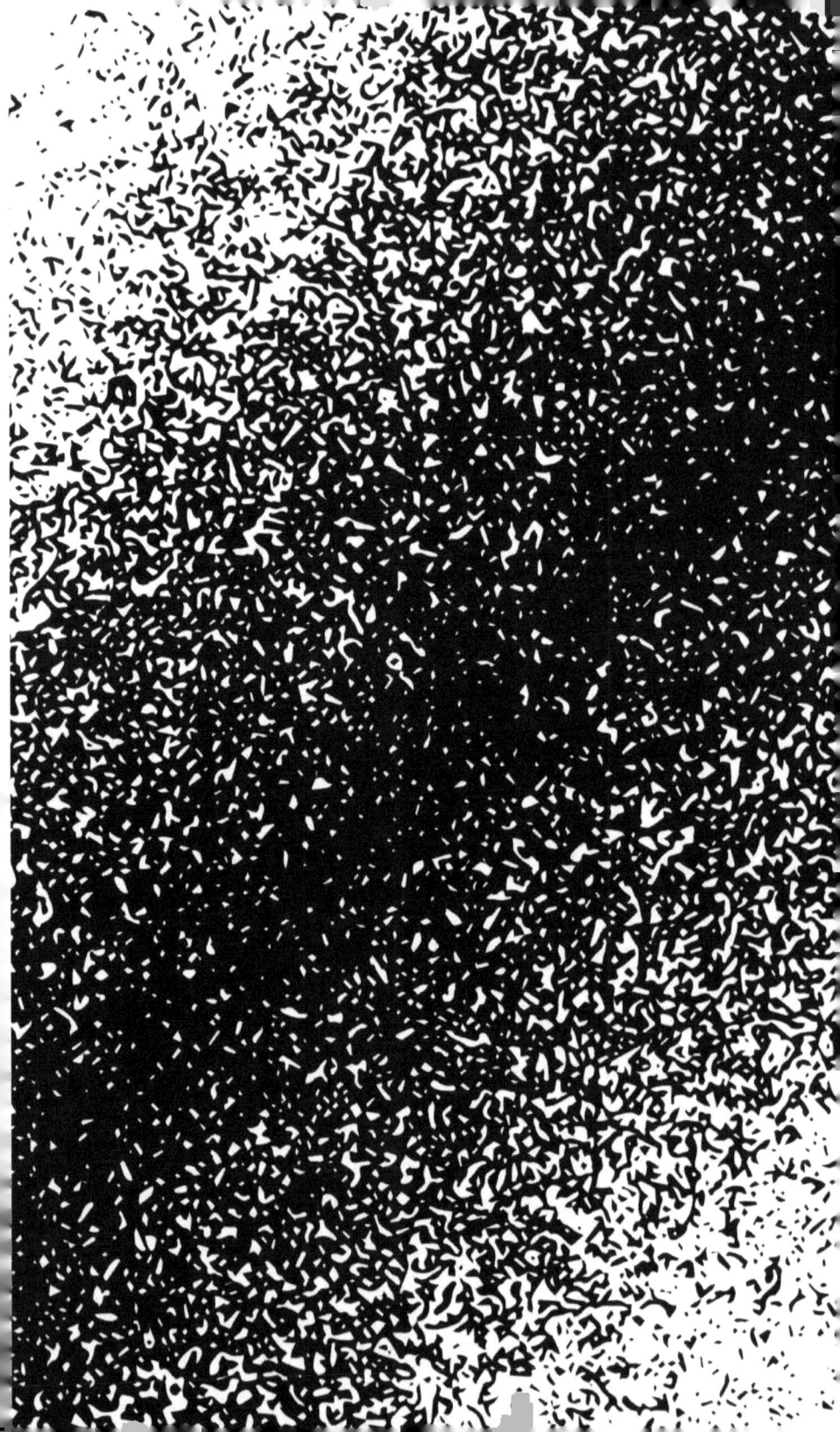

Unsavoriness

Faltered actions. Estranged friends following trendy attitudes aimed at disrespectful behavior, surviving alongside foes as we share a moment of calm with the very peer who've been disrupting our peace, attacking targets laced by an individual shrouded with faultiness... Counterfeits disgust me....

Blissfully said

S corched souls in search of redemption appeared in my peripheral, instantaneously, the moment I chose her heart.

Souls of the less fortunate, the envious, as well as the former lovers, seemed to stray from my path as I trekked on.

Bruises formed on their souls seemed relevant to my journey towards my future with her, who claimed I mattered to her mindset. Ascending into my place beside her kept my pulse at an all-time high as perspiration seeped through my pores more than ever, with every step closer to her heart.

Wails, shrieks, screams, shouts from the world were drowned out once she laid her gorgeous eyes on her future mate; all but one could be silenced as my focus was distracted for the first time.

Less speech

The vehicle backed up quickly to where I stood; she got out on the passengers' side; backing up to me slowly before turning. She smeared a perfect teardrop beneath my sight. She kissed me partially, blotting her eyes after she grabbed my fists and pleaded with me to understand that we didn't matter anymore as she hugged my torso.

I paused as she backed away from me, staring at me as I tossed the engagement ring I bought, watching her catch it with one hand and place it on her finger effortlessly. Reminding myself that this wasn't happening, I stared at her petite frame march backwards, carrying a few bags upstairs as our eyes met for the first time. Disappearing into the doorway of our life, she backed out, somehow gliding towards me before she retrieved her belongings. Reaching for my hand as I stated finally that I still loved her no matter what, before she passed me. She shook her head as she reached for the door behind her, taking a few steps to the side to get behind the door as I slammed it in her face with a partial smile.

She said my name after she knocked a few times as I paced back and forth regurgitating the wine; I used to share with her. I quickly hung up the phone after hearing her voice whisper before I hung it up as it began to ring several times, stopping as soon as I backed into the den. Wiping my eyes, I stopped as the tears jumped onto my beard and made their way up my cheeks and finding their way into the ducts whence, they came.

My frown disappeared as her picture did on my phone after she picked up hers, only to inform me she's been on my mind as I greeter her soft voice with mine before clicking over, back to the conversation I was having with my daughter who warned me of her malicious intent to scar my life as I tuned her out right before she slammed the phone down, hearing it ring as I heard it click right after I removed my thumb from the phone icon beneath her name....

Pretzel with pebbles

L oyalty comes at a price. It hovers over the mediocrity surrounding the masses, choosing only the official persons to matter in your life. However, you will encounter the unsavory, the ignorant, the envious as individuals with agendas unbecoming of their nature attempt to derail your life being that the life, they chose sealed itself behind the shame they've displayed over and over during your searching for better yourself.

These gnats deserve no attention; not to be crushed by the heel of your boot, not to be brushed away, but to understand that they never mattered towards your drive.

I no longer hold them in contempt. I pray for such individuals to find their way home.

If they're lucky, they'd be greeted by a warm pretzel with pebbles after it was retrieved from the driveway of their soiled minds

Hearsay

Whispers in the distance; moving quickly as the wind offers a lift to the nearest lobe meant to belittle the person referred to directly after a brief conversation with a stranger.

In this instance, a thought before replying never introduced itself to his mind as the world spun. The anonymity was priceless as he learned about trust and true friends. Distance played a role the closer they became, nearing the end of this conversation.

Moving with the breeze, they seem to back pedal towards the intersection where it all began; this time rewriting fiction as the name's being changed to protect the actual liar...

Considerable felon

She stole from me; she has no right, taking what doesn't belong to her. She should be considered a criminal for the damage she's done, carrying on her day as if nothing ever mattered to her. As my heartbeat slowed as she kept it in her purse while entertaining whoever she laid her beautiful eyes on.

Leaving clues for my eyes to decipher as I pursued a faint pulse as she smiled only a few feet from me while watching him in her peripheral. Controlling my emotions and laughing almost uncontrollably as tears race towards my beard, wiping my feelings aside as I stared at her.

Truths

The life I've lived turned out to be a full lie created by my actions, which coexisted behind mixed intentions for some time.

I've battled with these choices during the worst situations, forcing my hands into a negative manner. Striving alone within any means strewn in my peripheral, directing any memories to pause and refresh after I blink once I've dedicated attention.

Truth waited patiently in plain sight as my inconsistencies did their best to shield my focus simultaneously while their whispers grew louder.

Blinded with fear and envy, I've continued this tumultuous descent into a world of hate, followed by darkness once the shade introduced itself.

Looking up, I could still see my future as bright as can be, so I've opted to ascertain once I've began to ascend backwards.

Yearning to feel my future warmed from the sun's rays while staring down this dismal path, I've returned to my choice of happiness as I've denounced all hate with happiness.

Flawed last

I am broken, missing a fragment of my love as the front door to my future closes.

My heart aches a bit more than it did as her beautified face looked my direction for what seemed to be the last time. Revealing what I could only presume was a tear when I stumbled over my fears after my infidelities haunted me in a fashionable sequence.

I mourned. As she stripped me of my bond with her love, I suddenly regretted that kiss she had never gained from my attention after spotting me at my weakest point.

I dropped my valuables in an effort to bring her stability
as my fabled distraction prepared me for a dismal future
away from her love....

Weaponized scent

I am in no need to be loved as the trail of pain followed my every step, ruining my choices from future experiences to regretting past hopes.

Am I not a pure individual? lessened from deceitfulness while their cause meets every criteria set from a relaxed stance?

I'm focused; grinding my thoughts into a goal towards her, in an effort to relieve the tension of a single uneventful future destined for loneliness. But wait: a faint scent of vanilla softened summoned my dulled senses as she appeared on the horizon of my life.

Her pained focus alerted by my targeted posture as she entered my peripheral, slightly clouded vision as her heels made way towards the future she chose.

Whispered

She whispered from afar; gesturing her outstretched arms as if to welcome my mind as I approached her peripheral. Intentionally accepting her invitation to seduce my focus, I removed my sunglasses as her pupils dilated. She exhaled; once sensing my heart was lonely, yearning to pump vigorously. I held onto her soul, wanting everything offered by her willingness to love me as she accepted my pain.

Wrestling with my thoughts

Wrestling with my thoughts over being a gentleman and complimenting your gorgeous smile as you could perfect my stride once you accompany my airspace and decorate my lips with your nectar, kissing me. Wishing to participate in a bond to which my heart would be used as an entrance fee. I'd tour the very soul before my peripheral in amazement as your pulse somehow thumps to my very pace, being approached by your royalty.

I've dealt with the unsavory, the selfishness of said persons during this trial to which I've succumbed to, feeling as if I've been too damaged to love myself, let alone another woman.

Her freshly manicured hands grazing my dimples, making the hair on my beard straighter than usual....

Love hides from truth

Love redirects the pulse of he who infatuates himself beneath her stride as his legend pauses just enough for her to intervene with selflessness in his honor while celebrating his courtship among his peers and immortalizing his queen who hasn't adjusted with the very ring gifted to her as his mind accepted every flaw the world never noticed....

Balanced thoughts

Long were those days you'd swoon with my every step towards your soul; how I longed to stare into your smile as you blushed out loud whenever I'd catch a glimpse of perfection.

Short are the moments passing by each other demeanors, wondering if this actual love still exists as your stride entertains my ambition.

Thick are your impressions, somehow etched into my mind as the very heels worn by you marched simultaneously with my excited pulse.

Thin were the chances given as you strolled into the sunset, unable to secure a love unlike any other as my focus faded away.

Quick, with my intuition I've struck a nerve once I pinched your thoughts with melancholy from my soul in an attempt to gain attention as I covered your spinal cord, hoping for reciprocal love.

Dead as I felt your pulse cease once you slapped my dimple with an open fist, waving me off with the sudden breeze. Ouch.

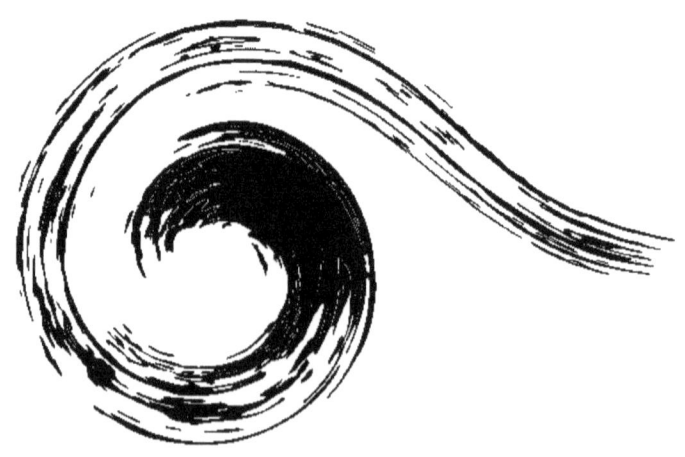

Infidelities combined

I don't know you; you look different in my peripheral. I can't feel you; it bothers the ridges of my fingertips. Talking to you muffles my senses as your soul seems uncanny, glazed with an unfamiliar coating which could've marked his property.

I can no longer linger by your scent; I tear knowing you've shared what was promised to our future. Clenching my heart as I walked away for the last time, I felt a breeze as he applauded my exit, knowing not what destruction lay in wait, as you pleaded with my shadows for reconciliation before his retreat.

I've lost the bond cherished solely while your tears soiled the allegiance created by your own free will, becoming the very decoration to his ego as he marked your place just beneath his last victim.

You've taught me what I can only describe as a respect for a path taken by the righteous as our lives entwined came apart at the seams.

Ours

Her pulse; as loud as it seemed, drowned out my thoughts once my attention was diverted.

My pressure slightly elevated once I've caught her attention simultaneously.

Her stride: interrupting my place of complacency as I've adjusted my soul to coexist with her highness's future, decorating my life with her perfection.

My approach into her palace greeted with a kiss as her hands wrapped themselves betwixt our thoughts, abducting my wellbeing along with my pulse, which beat to her every pace as she walked into my life...

Feelings Out Loud

Her relevance

She's Departed with my love; my tears are unassisted as they plunge towards the path created along with her alleged frustration as she hurried away from my sacrifices as I've attempted to secure my bond with her unhappiness, fathomed by no one.

I've cried briefly as her pulse ceased to exist alongside mine, causing this choice to echo in my mind somehow forever with the thought of any rekindling scarce.

She left my side for the last time, opting for a newer future laced with fortune and acceptance, as I've yearned for complacency as she used to caress my dimples after kissing my frontal lobe.

Her scent lingers still, which kept my love at bay for as long as I can remember, although her departure sealed my hopes alone, as her life continued in my absence. Whispering to my shadow, I've came to understand the darkness finally...

94

Who?

She doesn't know me. She glanced at my silhouette as my shadow interrupted her daylight, somehow irritating her as she read my mind.

She exhaled the more I chatted with her as I've tried to jog her memories with stories, nicknames, and favorite gifts.

She's so familiar to me as I've attempted to love her even while she's shrouded my thoughts with an uncanny smile during this attraction which kept my heart elevated...

Intentionally plain

E veryone sees your heart; few embrace it, others acknowledge your pulse as they carry on in an attempt to best you in your progression.

No one knows your intentions, let alone feelings, while engaging in mild dialogue poking at your cerebral cortex, searching for hints from within your domain.

Singling yourself out of the masses. Your stride is that of no one whispering in your peripheral, suddenly noticing the volume raised the further you get from that ashy vulgarity. They tried to matter being the so-called authors towards your path with innuendoes and rumors directing you towards a certain dismal epilogue.

You need not worry; they'll create one for the next person after you leave their sight......

I can

I can see you from the time my eyes focused.

I can appreciate your glossy lips wanting so badly to kiss mine as I stare into your lids, partially closed.

I can feel your bosom warmed as I wrap my soul around your smile.

I can imagine your pulse going awry to my every touch during the very encounter imagined.

I can taste your lips as you pucker in an attempt to sway my persuasion as I enhance my behavior in your shadow.

The stills in my life

I still love her; longing for her infamous scent of lilacs to caress my mind directly after the breath I've taken as I've approached the place we used to share.

I still adore her; watching her eyes brighten up with delight once her focus is directed at my attendance.

I still want her; fantasizing her hands running over my scalp as she'd kiss my dimples, staring into my soul and just enjoying my presence.

I still need her; feeling the cold pillow to my left as I've awakened from my fantasy beside her warmed love to a harsh reality which stung a bit.

I still cry for her; pleading before the mirror she'd frequent as she prepared herself to show the world who loved her more than anything before vanishing before my eyes.

I still wait for her return; forgetting to tell me she still loves me before kissing my lips.

I still want to answer the knock at the door; running downstairs in anticipation of love rekindled only to see her bestie with a package marked to me.

I stood extremely still as a lone tear escaped my control....

Deeper than my wounds

I am deeper than my wounds; you'd have to understand the scars in my mind created by your selfishness with every breath you've given towards the toxicity you've created between a bond once deemed unbreakable.

Please excuse my exit as I'll no longer utilize this companionship, which is draining my already empty soul, leaving this battered shell with little to no protection from the cruelty entrenched basically as far as my peripheral allowed.

I thank you, for I know now who you are....

Lost communication

Hi mom; I've been thinking about you a lot since your birthday as well as mine. I still tear during your holiday as I attempt to reminisce on what you meant to me as my birthday nears the horizon.

I smile at the rays peeking through my vision, prying my lids open as your silhouette seems to guide my love towards the heavens, enabling my tears to glide towards my beard, pausing slightly as they cover my dimples during this moment of joy loving you the way everyone you've came to be appreciated.

Just thanking you for your role as the first woman I've ever loved. A special godsend....

Sculptor awakening

Inconspicuously, I felt her softened hands caress my thoughts as she blinked several times in an attempt to get my attention, strutting her smooth body right past my suddenly visible dimples.

I reached for her soft side, not anticipating a well-manicured hand greeting my subtle advances. She placed a hold on to my soul, long enough to plant a kiss while experiencing an unusual thump beneath my skin as my pulse erupted just above her lips during the moment, she decided to taste the skin right against my jugular.

She deserves that right. Glancing at my shoulders and admiring the scent of a sweetened cologne as she found her hands wrapping themselves partially around my body, synchronizing with her pulse in time to admire my stride as I made myself comfortable behind her irises.

Faults

Reasons for trust shouldn't exist as I look to my left, noticing my friends' departure from my circumference as I wonder at my future, unguarded from their protection as they reappeared in the stands applauding my demise which was thwarted by the friends on my right, barricading my life within theirs... only the appreciated need not ask for they are greatly appreciated for such actions...

Darkest blue

My life: reasoning with my reflection as he begs me not to bring my wallet with me nor my phone. Fearing an onslaught as I concealed both within the folds of my jacket, I argue back as my thoughts reconvene on the curb before their aim, shouting obscenities daring me to draw my weapon of choice which could probably brighten up the shadow of doubt surrounded by their peers as I've been fitted to a description based on a hue gifted to my life....

Sound of my tears

The pitter patter almost distracted my thoughts during this time once she came to mind.

Her smile whenever I'd stare at her from afar always cheered me up, no matter the circumstance. I placed a single rose before her full name etched out as I remembered the happiness she'd displayed although she was gone too soon, clenching the thoughts of never talking to her ever again as the grip on my past allowed me to reminisce on who I could say was almost perfect.

I find myself fighting back tears, knowing that I celebrate her usually yearly, allowing myself one-sided conversation with her soul as I usually feel a breeze on my shoulders as if she attempted a walkthrough from within my thoughts.

Wiping my brow as I cleared my throat aggressively, somehow waiting for confirmation from no one to my knowledge. I whispered her name, as I could feel tears streaming from my ducts within seconds as I yearn for her to speak my name one last time, drowned out by the pitter patter.

Reminisced

I have been here before; familiar scenery, the scent of lilacs faintly grazes my nostrils as I reminisced. Recalling every step from here on scared me, wondering why I would've been able to do so. Her scent gets stronger, forcing my future towards her intent as tears shed unexpectedly from my very own ducts.

I felt her whispers as they blew across my beard, reaching my lobes in a timely fashion. Remembering the conclusion suddenly, I opened the door as he knocked on the opposite side. I smiled as she stood beside him, reassuring her I've always respected her choices even though I wasn't included.

Noticing a scent unfamiliar to my senses, I scoffed as he collected her belongings and exited my peripheral, leaving a trail of mistakes before her dulled senses.

I looked her direction and wished her the best as she picked up the aroma suddenly, remembering my loyalty as I closed my door to her surprised face.

I've been here before; I've closed that chapter of my life a while ago.

Camouflage

Camouflage: used in the right manner, one gains the advantage against his opponent. Alleged conspiracies surrounding said actions shroud true intentions; therefore, once they've been spotted, the damage is done.

I've kept my friends closer than anyone.

I've trusted throughout my tumultuous life.

I've shook hands with my enemies and gave my friends head nods as if I should beware of their glares aimed at my shoulder blades.

Don't believe me? You don't have back problems; you have wounds from the world knowing your dilemmas as narrated from your rider or family.

I standalone; against the wolves, the mediocrity, the meek, the rumors, the envious, the audacious, the ones seeking refuge, the last one to put their hand out. Only one hand, so you don't see the serrated blade to your immediate right.

Shattered souls worship your downfall. Keep shuffling to their left until you understand their purpose...

Food for thought

If I loved her with all my heart, should she have been afraid?

If I have her my soul, would that be enough to fuel her love or lack thereof?

If I trusted her long before I've decided to decorate her finger as my better half, does she deserve the right to humiliate my feelings on a whim?

If I decided to welcome her into my life, should she be gratified?

If we come to a crossroads during our time together, would it be fair to reminisce on what we've built rather than choosing separate paths?

If I lost everything important to me, would I be able to count on her guidance and love to boost my drive to maintain?

If I am no longer able to support her in the way needed, will she understand time, or replace my loyalty with uncertainty?

If I greeted her with roses, would she rejoice before she pricks her finger or weep as the aroma finds her nostrils as I enter her peripheral?

If I've shared my love with someone other than her, would I be as special to her as the scent confuses the atmosphere surrounding her hallway?

If I do love her, will it last in her mind as she watches my happiness grow by the day, even though I've held her responsible for my heart?

If I've asked her to marry me, would she say yes?

If......

Hidden scars

Badages running out; leaking profusely as I attempted to locate my adversaries heavily armed.

Looking around, I see no one close enough to inflict damage without my knowing. Blinded by false smiles and naysayers, I strafed past the lot of them as the feel of cold steel pierced the area just below my shoulder.

Spinning around in time to see an old friend released their grip, almost giggling to themselves as I stumbled into reality. I froze as she shrugged her shoulders with no regards towards my relevancy. Spotting another foe to her left, recognizable to my focus as well as she was, before asking for more information to use against me.

Ignoring the attempts to further scar my reputation or livelihood, I smiled at their determination once I've realized the blood on my shoulder blades didn't belong to me.

Wishful thinking

I used to wish I was relevant to her,

I used to want to host her smile with mine,

I used to trail her progress with my pupils,

I used to worship her every step as she trekked in my mind,

I used to hold her bosom as close as possible while admiring her pores as her scent kept my mind awry with pleasure.

I used to serenade her as she sat before me, marveling my affection as she massaged my mind with her pulse.

I used to say her name as my life revolved between the syllables of her name.

I used to sacrifice my entire being no matter the cost just to watch her pretty smile form before me.

I no longer consider my life irrelevant, as I've secured her heart beside me as my better half...

I thought...

I thought I heard your pulse as the slugs exited your Glock, destined to tour my cavity as soon as your intuition kicked in, hoping for a righteous kill justifying any suspicion you've kept hidden from your report.

I thought I heard your radio as you called for reinforcements the moment my body hit the pavement, during which you shouted racial epithets towards my position besides your shadow, watching my life attempt to leave through the very eyes focused on yours.

I thought I heard your footsteps, louder than my heartbeat, as you seemed to stuff a loaded cell phone into my breast pocket after you turned my warm body aside, leaving your prints smudged on my blood-soaked hoodie.

I thought I saw your look of fear host a smirk, thinking about your next shift as your partner produces a piece of chalk, creating an outline around my body as he chuckled at your attempt to falsify my demeanor to which you claimed I didn't matter to this world.

I thought I heard your body cam switch on as people gathered, pulling out their phones and accusing you repeatedly as you retreated beside your fellow assassins, refusing local eye contact among your fellowship as your lie becomes subjected towards scrutiny created behind the sight of flares ignited as the sirens drowned out the very thoughts of anarchy as the crowd grew impatient during your decision to claim self-defense.

I thought I felt your eyes watching my blood-soaked body cool off as my soul appeared to soar above this crime scene as you intended to stick to your so-called story.

I thought I saw your expression change once I coughed up protein, disclaiming your very diction as you felt the pain of my peers once your cuffs clicked behind your very back......

Fractionated

I've assaulted the masses with mediocrity as I searched to become a factor in her life.

I've lowered my expectations with impatience as my wants outweighed my hearts' desire.

I've found myself at the mercy of the selfish, the unfaithful, or most abusive.

I've known these feelings as I've searched for her, reemerging as my mind loses focus from this distraction.

I've been impressed by her advertising techniques with just her gorgeous soul accompanied by the sweetest smile.

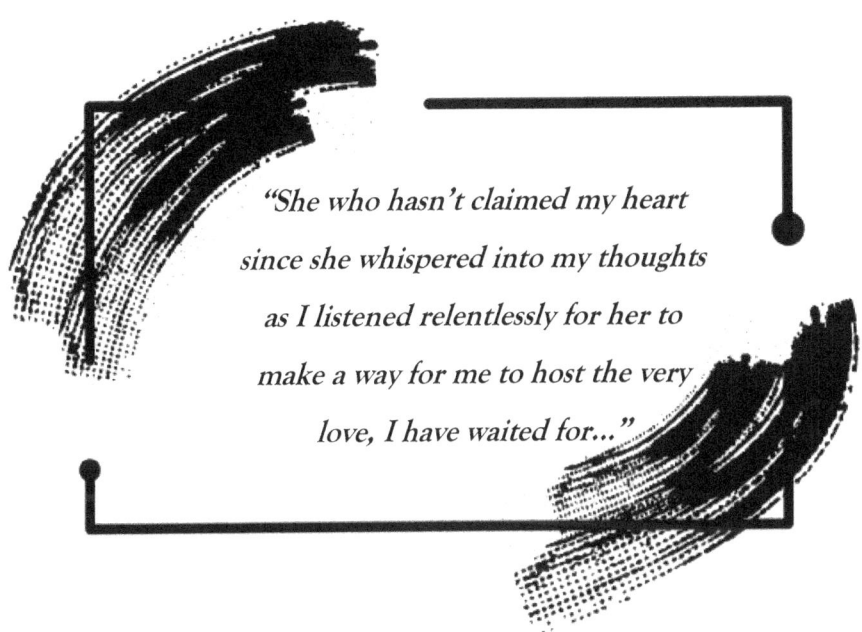

"She who hasn't claimed my heart

since she whispered into my thoughts

as I listened relentlessly for her to

make a way for me to host the very

love, I have waited for..."

Evaporation

The trust is gone; forgiveness is a must as I've replaced your mediocrity with the life I've led previous to this downtrodden behavior you've introduced me to.

Readjusting my direction as I've tossed the fork in the road aside, I've listened to the mud slosh beneath my shoes once I've created my path beside said utensil.

Your tears of manipulation drying up as my choice welcomed the rays of a brightened future beneath the sun. As I wiped my tear-stained shirt, I felt the weight of your selfishness lifted with your grasp loosed, allowing me to sprint towards the truthful destiny I've longed for....

Bruised accomplice

I hate you; I watched you smile as he kissed your hand simultaneously, as the flowers I held escaped my grasp, plunging towards certain death.

My tears fought before my ducts before letting go once both dimples appeared when he adorned your shoulders with wreaths, appreciating your heart the exact way I planned to as you motioned for me to accompany your stride by his side right as my irises focused on a dismal future watching your love gloat to my meagerness sealed my pulse into a mild coma when you said yes.

Assumptions

The piercing of this silence shook the boldest individuals as their bond was interrupted.

The shrieks were uneasy to comprehend as his frown shaped the dismantled course before him.

Assumptions led the path astray, laced with infidelities as they both refused their roles towards a reconciled love.

His stoic look displaying actual pain coupled with tears, certified the ending of this bond as he covered his face before her excursion into uncertainty.

You've lost me

The hardest thing to see is the truth when you reveal your soul. Fear of losing what you never had comes full circle as trust bypasses you unbeknownst of your true intentions.

Feeling the ridges of your fingertips basically slip away from my reality clarified your reason for lacking as my heart yearned for a reconciliation.

You've lost me; haven't you? I'm out of tears as they've been transferred throughout my soul, exiting numerous pores decorating my tired body. Sweating profusely, I stared at my future as it invited my hopes towards a next chapter of my life minus the stress from the only one that mattered to my attendance.

DEDICATION

Thank you, God Almighty, for allowing my talents to reach new highs.

I'd like to thank Mark & Leditra Stenett, Maya, Ajay with Zachary, Jeff & Lisa Masse, Mason (fam for life). Amir & Usein, Aneasha & Ashanti (I love you more than anything on this planet). Sierra, Noah, Nicholas, Nyla with Latoya (RIP), Lydia, Lisa, Shanda, Joemel, Joemel jr, Jayla & Jordyn, Heather & Jean Belfort, Alfred (love you pop). Raymonde (love & miss you RIP). Uncle Gerry & aunt Shirley, Uncle Peter (RIP), Natalie & Kati Guerrier. Dyna & Neheme. Savannah & Xavier. Shariff Allah (didn't forget you, big bro!!).

Wayne (RIP). Anthony & Kimberly. Bryan Stevenson, Leslie, Mr. & Mrs. Ashley. Averil, Gary, Kenny, Garfield, Nerlande (I love you a million times over). Aaron, Tyler, Tim, Sarah, Jonathan, Stacey Innocent, Gordon Pryce, Steven (Pit) & Phil. James & John B Codrington, Kal Mitchell & Sharon. Erika & Storm Snoddy. Ravi Marwah, Shirlena, Dena, Vaukesha, Guerrier, Denise & Latelle Ashe. Barbara & Cathiana Sansaric. Majestic, Tasha & Tara. Rob Hunter, Manny Kieth, Marjorie & Jirka. Yanique & Jean. Benjamin, junior Lacombe, Yolanda, Michelle, Andre, Kieth, Alnethia, Marv & Neet Bowman. Kieth & Kesha Perrin. Marcia Parks, Tina Parks & Kesha Stoddart. Maria Aduke Alabi, Messfin Tafari Savage, Alfredo & Yusmila.

Avila, Shawn Brown (RIP), Diquan (RIP) & Debbie Pearson (RIP). Marjorie & Melvin Coeur, Andrea Dyer, Karen, Johnnie Mcray, Cynthia, Marky & Leatrice. Poppy, Imani & Urijah Jeanbaptiste. Ray (RIP), Frank Ian & Sandra (RIP). Terah, Charisse, Mason & Ethan Sapp. Wise, Mary, Shamel, Shakim, Maj, Kim, Stretch (RIP). Ronnie & Addy. Tyleeki, Shandora, Tyleah, Sha & Eboni Browning. Tracey Gamble (RIP), Zendon Hamilton, Chudney Gray, Anthony Glover, Sharif Fordam, Sharon, Nitra (RIP), Qiana (RIP), Lashawn (RIP), Robert "Peedy" Jones, Tishura Dalrymple, Simone & Gabrielle Duzant. Aniyah Johnson, Alaysia (Lay-Lay) Duzant (I love you a thousand times over).

Anthony Duzant (RIP), Kim, Jerome & Alton Wilson. Juwanna & Jamel Roberts. Chantel & Manny Chambers. Will, Nicole, Natalie & Nia Hammond.

Janel Rodgers, Adam & Judette Lespinasse. Barbara, junior, Cathiana Sansaric, Kiera Weaver, Josiah & Justin Wood. Stevie & Aliyah Johnson. Mathew Threadgill, Narada & Nikki Watson. Sweet Koko, Alicia Brown, Pumpkin & the entire staff at Rockaway Fish House.

Manny Kieth, Alberto & Karen Modesto. Gail, Larry, Mark & Sakina Shannon. Dion McCain, B. Dot Miller, Larry, Javanna, Orin & Anthony Anderson. Lena, Naomi Lacombe, Towan Hopkins, Isaiah Wilson, Latoya Phillip, Terrell & Threa Taylor. Monisha, Monique (love you so much). Nicky Williams (always ready to support from Connecticut). Isaiah Wilson (coolest guy). Rosemary, Ralph, Brandon Calvert (thank you for your support).

Shalona Brown, Fawnita (RIP) & Hev Lunn. Tierre (RIP) & Twyla Pettaway. Thomas Rollins, Gerald, Diana, Georgia, Mr. & Mrs. Christie. Kim White & Yolanda Pruitt. Robin, Sean (anchorman). Will & Erica Townsend. Alfredo & Yusmila Avila. Parris Morris, Delissa Kato-Taylor, Bobby Kato, Coco (I need a drink, please).

Damion, Kyle, Devon, Devin & Kyra Mollison. Darrin, Karen, Joanne Carlie, Okini, Job & Audrey Reid (my love a thousandfold to your being) …….

EDITOR NOTES:
We accept the excessive use of contraction in some poems to respect the poet's style and edit the collection without missing the natural rhythm of each poem. The ellipsis in this content is mostly used to show a pause in speech without missing its formality. The paragraph arrangement -one paragraph per poem- is intentional and required by the poet.

.